Mixed MESSAGES

Mixed MESSAGES
Judith Lapadat

CAITLIN PRESS INC.

Copyright ©2002 Judith C. Lapadat

All rights reserved. No part of this publication may be reproduced, stored in a retrieval system or transmitted in any form, by any means without prior permission of the publisher, except by a reviewer who may quote a passage in a review, or in the case of photocopying or othe reprographic copying, a licence from ACCESS (The Canadian Copyright Licensing Agency), 1 Yonge Street,Toronto,Ontario M5E 1E5.

Published by
Caitlin Press Inc.
Box 4460, Quesnel BC, V2J 3J4
Prince George, BC V2N 2S6

Cover and interior layout and design by ptpublishing
Cover art created by Judith Lapadat: front "October Afternoon"; back "Spring Breakup at Cottonwood Island"
Author photo taken by photographer Stephan A. Lapadat

National Library of Canada Cataloguing in Publication Data

Lapadat, Judith Colleen, 1956-
 Mixed messages / Judith Lapadat.

Poems.
ISBN 0-920576-96-6

I. Title.
PS8573.A61M59 2002   C811'.6   C2002-911300-8
PR9199.4.L37M59 2002

The Canada Council for the Arts
Le Conseil des Arts du Canada

BRITISH
COLUMBIA
ARTS COUNCIL
Supported by the Province of British Columbia

Caitlin Press Inc. gratefully acknowledges the financial support of the Canada Council for the Arts for our publishing program. Similarly, we acknowledge the support of the Arts Council of British Columbia.

Printed in Canada by Houghton Boston Printers and Lithographers

*I dedicate this book to
Katherine, Erica, and Alex
-- companions on my life's journey.*
-Judith C. Lapadat

CONTENTS

MIXED MESSAGES #1
The Spider of Convention 2
Down 3
Baby Food 4
Ice 5
Existential Math 6
Fool Hen 8

IN MEMORIAM
My Eyes 10
Our Luck 11
Time's Neckhold 12
Those Patient Shoes 13
rot 14
The Kind of Man 15
Seeking his Scent 17
Song of the Suicide Survivor 18
Widow's Life 19
Long Day 20
Lights Out 21
Lost Hair 22
Memory Deconstruction 23
Delete 24
His Marks 25
39 26
The Semiotic Fox 27

MIXED MESSAGES #2
Her Dad 30
Baby 31
Dream Ghost 32
Tick tick tick 33
Guilt 34
Thin Edge 35
Secretaries 36
Song lines 37
Statue Man 38
History 39

KUMQUAT POEMS
Separate Cages 42
Two Rings 43
Dreaming in Colour 44
Red Flowers 45
Following the Rules 46
Kumquat 47
Hopeless Hope 48
Exchange 49

MIXED MESSAGES #3
Troll 52
Boundaries 53
Giving Voice 54
Mommy Medusa 56
List of Rules 57
Still Shots 59
Colour 60
September Eleventh 61
Slipping Inside 62
I Am Old 64
Broken Dishes 65
Travelling Forward 67

POINTS NORTH
Written-Upon Woman 70
Valley Of My Childhood 72
December 25 74
Sculpture 75
Left Behind 76
Bees Among the Canes 78
Stolen Moment 79
Haiku for October 80
Restless Feet 81
November Grey and Black 82
In a Swamp 83
Erasures 84

Mixed MESSAGES #1

The Spider of Convention

Furry spider
big as a hat
sits on my head
Is it my head
Black spider
sits on my passion
Is it my passion
The spider of convention
I mention it
in passing to
my flighty-winged friends
buzzing by
not tied
"Hey Jude
nice hat"

Down

    Down
down down down the watery bathtub hole I go, no
                              time left
   sucked round and round so quickly down in
   earth's vortex
       where is that wise brown-eyed baby
                            gone
      that long-haired girl with a book
     gone
        lover of a bearded man
                   gone
        angry busy mother
       gone
         teacher writer
             gone
         so quickly
         old hag
         going
         goin
          g
          o
          n
          e
          .

Baby Food

My plump cream-fed baby
fed by a mother
who is fed by the food
of the bony mother
of the bony baby
who has no milk
whose mother has no food

Sucking weak at wasted breast
Eating at your mother's rack of bones
Will you grow up, bony babe
to pick food in fields
to send to me
and my sweet-cheeked girl
who swivels and scowls
in front of a mirror
cursing her dimples and swelling breasts
curve of belly and rounded thighs
While you fist your finger bones
into the gnawing ache of hungry belly
Now carrying a child

Ice

I have lived my life on ice
Skied, skated, driven on ice
Sped down the fall line
Listened to the hiss
grunt and scratch, set an edge
Don't catch an edge, go over the edge
Found that centre of balance to leap and land
precisely
carve a perfect arc with an inside edge
and smiled
as I steered into the skid
accelerated
didn't let my wheels catch the shoulder slush
suck me into ditch litter
dirty snow
bodies to the side, receding behind
a popped out knee
a shattered ankle
cold metal wrapped around a head injury
box of brain soup
brittle bones and broken hips.
I am tired,
old.
I want something solid and slow
like a rocking chair
where I will rest and watch my children
speed away down hills of ice.

Existential Math

A line is the shortest distance between two points
invisible points
that exist placed in space
by your belief.

Your belief defines an invisible line
a sequence of many more points than two
standing side by side
they have no thickness
no size at all
so there really must be millions
for even the shortest line.

How do you know which two
define the line?

And if the line is imaginary
(let's say you refuse to believe)
what does that say about engineers
and bridges?

Oh, and I forgot to mention
that *real lines* go on forever
all those zillions of points
a whole infinity
used up on a single line
none left to define
another line or two
unless there is more than one infinity
or imagination doesn't have to make sense
in the case of lines.

Considering that lines aren't big enough
to even be there
they get into our thoughts a lot.

We try to manufacture lines
in roads and houses and art.

We put letters on a page
as if they were points on a line
and throw sounds into the air
like lines to someone's ear.

We imagine
that we live a line of time
pretend the points are real
and think we know which two
define the line.

Fool Hen

The fool hen with tiny stupid eyes
sits picking bran and needles
from the brain behind my painted face.
She tightens the rope
at my neck
chokes my words, pecks my cheeks
Flutters her grousey feathers
in my breathless chest
until panicked
I run, scrabbling gravel
into the road.
Easy meat
for men with guns.

IN Memoriam

My Eyes

My eyes, always dark, are now black
holes that burn
when you meet my gaze.
My agony is a beacon
attracting your own pain.
Turn away from the images of death
my face presses against
my eyes turn towards.
You see a small woman
white-faced children clinging in tableau
silent, solitary, struggling through a void;
We see nothing, hear nothing
but visions of our dead love
husband, father
dead by his own hand.
Ashes on our lips
Screaming in our heads
Crying in our hearts
in this terrible silence.

Our Luck

We always said we were lucky together
Together we'd make it.
It's the accretion of little things –
broken toilet
job rejection
unreturned call
That tells us our luck has changed.
Everyone turns away from a dying man
Seeing the flurry of appointments
applications, and sudden projects started and dropped
not as floundering of a man going under
but as marks of a loser.
So you held the pain in
secret whirlpool sucking you down
until the only solution seemed to be
a rope around your neck
in the garage in the afternoon
while the children slept.
And I too stood by
helpful words half-hearted
We always made it through before
Weren't you big? Weren't you strong?
And now I am tossed up alone
in the backwash of broken toilet
broken children
broken trust.

Time's Neckhold

After your death, dear Love
I scream on a tightrope
with children
endure
stares theories hugs
Then plastered flat on a barren deathscape
immobilized by gravity
each muscle moved by desperate will
exhausted with despair
in halls and filing cabinets of bureaucracy
appointments phone calls forms
suicide clause, don't qualify, physician's statement, police report
The house is silent
the music has stopped
the bed is cold
Nightmares own my sleep.
Caught in Time's neckhold
marched through this
I learn it is time
to take responsibility for my own life
make choices for love and life
and shun the twin traps:
technology's machine of the daily grind
and entertainment addition
promises escape and delivers isolation
No longer will I sleepwalk through my days
too distracted to care
too cowed to scream "bullshit!"
The death engineers have taken you
but I will not give in to them
I am fighting for love
I am fighting for life.

Those Patient Shoes

It was his shoes
that caused the pain in her chest
sudden in-breath
      then forget to breathe.

Those patient shoes
worn leather casings
      for his big flat feet
in the closet, by each door
Black industrial gumboots, for gardening
      now dusted grey.

She couldn't stoop to pick them up
to garbage can or goodwill
though she rehearsed the act
in the clear light of her mind's vision
      several times a day.

Shoes shaped by his weight and sweat
run down at heels, worn soles
neatly side-by-side
She sees the cobwebs forming
      adds a silent scream.

His feet have been cremated
      shoes remain.

rot

a small woman
dull eyes, flat black
lips pursed from sucking lemons
or is it bleach
to clean the bloody stain
on hands that didn't hold
his bright spirit
ran through her fingers
a greasy stain
now ash, now dust
from her cracked and bleeding lips
a drop, two drops
splatter with a silent puff
busy spiders already spinning
webs over his shoes, his tools
soft heart of rot
spreading from the inside
of fruit
children stretched tight
and bright over silent decay
clawing at each other's eyes
when you look away

Judith Lapadat

The Kind of Man

He was the kind of man
who carried his baby on his hip
while he cooked ham and lentil stew
in a bright clean kitchen
on a winter afternoon.

He was the kind of man
who played angry music very loud
danced with his daughters
flinging them to the ceiling
catching them again
while they shouted out the words.

He was the kind of man
who read the classics
and talked about
philosophy and world events
at dinner parties.

He was the kind of man
trusted by elderly people
who sought his help
he took the time to care
about each story.

He was the kind of man
who loved his wife
with bright passion
urged her to fight
and have faith in herself.

He was the kind of man
who panicked when black bands
of depression cinched his soul
and fear clouded his vision
who, in a frenzy, hung himself
while the children played in their rooms
on an afternoon in June.

Seeking his Scent

Like a crazed animal
she scurries
eyes wild, hair plastered back, nostrils flaring
to every closet, his truck, his pillow
seeking his scent.
Dead ashes in a box
yet his pheromones remain
a whack on memory's temple
or subtle shading of eddies
lifted as she crosses a room.
She finds him in the sweat
soaked in the straps of the baby backpack
on so many day trips
while she carried the drinks and lunch.
She finds him in his red wind-breaker
a cheap one that didn't breathe
but held the moisture in.
She finds him in the bucket seat
of his little brown truck
mixed with the oily smell
from its sewing machine motor
that took us to Yellowstone while it burned
and to Banff and back.
She finds his smell
still in the lonely pillow
on his side of the bed.

Song of the Suicide Survivor

When you were walking into that dark land
you did not tell me of the bitter possibility
that filled your heart, your eyes – why?
As you turned to that bleak horizon
discordant dirge pounding in your head
until the sound seemed irresistible
this sunlit world of mundane everyday became a dream
my love a pretty memory catching at your wrists
frail threads to sweep aside.
Did you want to protect me
from the pain you embraced?
Or was it my respect for you
you wanted to preserve?
Seductive shadows enclosed you
Those bloody lips left greedy marks all around your neck.
At the last you turned away from us
this world of light and joy and love
and ran, ran, ran
hands over ears
humming or screaming
to your final moment.
And I wonder if you kept your grisly secret
only to make sure
I would not save you.

Widow's Life

Caught
knees & elbows
ankles & wrists
Crushed in these tumbled pick-up sticks
that don't stay picked up.
Oppression of detail
I boil the kettle, NOT
reaching through steam.
I butter bread for you and you, NOT
putting the butter knife on the cloth.
I pick up toys
hundreds of toys
again, again
stoop & straighten
Their bright colours lie
Happy happy!
Gifts from the devil
to test how far these joints can stretch
on the torture rack of motherhood.
Wanton
they throw the toys around
again
Can they break something, spill something?
Squash or squirt something?
Smear greasy fingers on the wall
play with plugs in sockets
tip their grape juice off the table
try to reach through steam.
And I am running, running
to grab them in time
fetch this or that
wipe noses or juice.
Throw me in a bag
sew my lips to your nipple
and take me away from here.

Long Day

Past spring equinox
we are spinning into light
long day, short night
lips crack, eyes burn
meat left out
beads with grease bubbles
curls up at edge
beg the cruel sun for sleep
trapped under its bored
beneficent gaze
unblinking O
needles brilliant torture
into wakeful eyes
bug on a pin
spinning into perpetual daylight
summer solstice
takes neck in hand
wraps tight
and dangles
death a kind of sleep
a kind of darkness.

Lights Out

The moon was round and yellow
low over the trees
in the early part of the evening
Then later rose higher
blue-edged clouds scudding across its face.
Dry leaves clattered like tiny bones
Lifted and swirled behind the heels
of children running in flapping capes
down sidewalks and through ditches
blind in the dark until they reached
the next circle of light.
I ran too
laughing with my girls
calling out to passing groups
in that magic night.
Sometimes remembered to be a mom
"Look both ways before you cross!
Don't cut over the neighbour's lawn!"
You were home in the warm house
handing out treats.
That was the Halloween before you died.
Now another Halloween chills my bones
skeletons, tombstones and walking dead
symbols of death appropriated
for children's fun
innocent couriers in spirit garb
blind to their bleak message.
Is your spirit curling through the garden?
Are your ashes dancing
on this October wind?
The lights are out at our house.

Lost Hair

I sit down at the keyboard
on the ergonomic chair that
stolidly upheld your weight
on its single stainless post
so many hours.
So many times I sat here after you
heart clutched in my chest
to see your hair
shed over the keyboard
lost hair the ebbing of life
over this endless work
a balding man
in a sunless room.
Now I sit, stare
not one hair
is in among the keys
the chair seems spritely
I have put in a window.
Your hair, head, all of you
dead.
I yearn for the pathos
of hair on the keyboard
your work forever
incomplete.

Memory Deconstruction

So tiny
this little picture…
you and me by the tent, frying trout
after miles of choking dust
that blistered general store
crouched at the foot of clear-cut hills
its back to the lake
where we could buy
baloney white bread spinners bait
and stand outside eating red licorice
in the oily yard
of broken machines and weeds
…shrinking.
Going, disappearing
almost gone.
An arch needs two pillars
A baby needs two sets of genes
This memory needs you
to share it
I cannot hold onto it
alone.
Reality deconstructed
picture shrinks
losing it,
you.

Delete

It's time to be sensible now
set up blind dates for her
say the word
suicide
without averting eyes.
But never never say his name.

What more could I want
than a warm plush cat
asleep at the foot of my empty bed.
Never never say his name.

Rush from school to friends
lessons sports popcorn
Mom this Mom that.
Never never say Dad's name.

Car accident or cardiac arrest
we'd write miss-you poems
in memoriam
for the local rag.
Colleagues would make tribute.

But you pressed delete
erased yourself.
So we never never say your name.

His Marks

This finger
ringless
bears your ring's indentation
a circle of wasted flesh.
You broke our vows
death did us part.
Fleshy impression forever marks
like silver belly bands
your children borne
my body marked.
I inhaled your expended air
shared sweat and spit
gave brain and soul.
Though I remove the ring
my body remembers
who I am is partly you
so little left
not the legacy you intended.

39

Thirty-nine
end of the line
for you
Older than you now
I'm over the hill
in your ashpit
back forty
Horizon a dirty trick
Black words backwards
stuck in the now
walking
walking
deathplots to the side
quicksand
slow slog
pick my steps
safety as thin as string
catastrophe as bland as cheese
guilt as round and silent
as a log
Older, pinched, sad
walking
walking
Heavy steps
in these sturdy urns

The Semiotic Fox

A man
drove his family van
to the edge
rocky bank of rushing
muddy spring run-off river
flood stressed willows
persist
thoughts of fish
drowning thoughts insist:
brown water inhaled.
Then the semiotic fox is there
his fox confirms
ritualizes
the death vision.
It is out of his hands
part of a larger pattern
signs and symbols
willow, water
rocks and fox
cold dreams of fish
wishes rushing
oblivion
nose mudstopped
flesh soft and cold
fish eyes unblinking
just a sunpicked pattern
of bones
on the stone bank
river running down the valley.
Fox sits
grins into the sunset
with yellow eyes.

Mixed MESSAGES #2

Her Dad

Butter wouldn't melt
on your icicles
when you come
poking
prying
sliding slivers
into my still bleating
blood red

Hard
icy shards
fingernails
or silver wires
thread my arteries
seeking

Hot
tears on frostbitten
passion
never to talk

Hate to hate
you
sheep maker
lamb beater
Bad. Bad.

Baby

Baby
belly ball
So cold out here
Sharp edges and eyes
I'd swallow my kitten
like Saint-Exupery's boa
safe inside
(if I didn't step
in front of a bus)
Baby elephant
would you tell
of your confinement
when you tired of snug
and longed to run
trumpet danger
This worm cannot contain
an elephant

Dream Ghost

The remembered fear of starting awake
to see a ghost in flowing white
silent at the foot of the bed
drifting away
imprint of a cold hand
against my sweaty cheek
perhaps a kiss
from lips dry as dust
in the dead of night
is understood
now that I am the one who floats
long after midnight
to the beds of sleeping children
kiss them once more
stroke their cheeks
I'm cold and hollow-eyed
in the dark house
Precious night hour
stolen from greedy work and sleep
transforms mother into
dream ghost.

Tick tick tick

I am afraid of ladders, balconies and roofs
I might jump
A normal fear
like cringing from gangs of smoking boys
piss-pants men in litterblown parks
four a.m. phone calls
footfalls in an alley.
Tick tick tick the night-time clock
ticks away my time
screams in the morning, get up!
Insomnia can make you crazy.
When the big hand squeezes my heart
will that red squirrel relax
fight
or love the fall
flying just once from the top of the cliff?
One day the battery runs out
limp hands like noodles
we don't know the time.

Guilt

Guilt
is a mouthful of aluminum
headful of shoulds
should heed
foil
shrouds
like little bundles
round the egg-sac
sickly white-faced
mouthful of couldn'ts
cozy packages
emissaries
from mouth to heedless
brain
chanting
shoulds and shouldn'ts
headin back
to hedonistic
flagellation
sliced tongue
tastes bloody foil
failed to convince
convicted

Thin Edge

Little leaf quivers a
      lone
in the big chatter
shrieks and hugs of flesh-padded
too-tight bras
pink knit sweat
hers.
      Brittle
thin as a cross-section
in this crosstalk of potluck
      "Chris'
sakes I hate these socials."
Women being exclusive women
leave no chinks
for the thin edge of the
      witch
left smiling at air
reading labels, last year's lists
on the homely bulletin board
which at least makes an attempt
to communicate.

SECRETARIES

Thin lips like a cat
carnivorous teeth
secretary at her desk

Sharks circle the pool
want to rip flesh
Boss keeps her door closed

Former Boss
(scurrying little fellow
in a fuzzy brown suit)
gave the nice girls mums
on Secretary's Day

Never declawed
she paints her nails red or black
clickety click
clickety click

Lazily circles
the sea-green pond
scarcely a ripple among
sleek girls with yellow eyes
poised unblinking at their desks

Ready for action
waiting for blood
playing the game

Song lines

blue avenue tells
secret dirt
dark page pronounces
song lines

summer morning here sounds
off
tendrils work, consume
dark song lines
     song lines

slender minute grows
builds wind
winds secret work
wants morning sound
mourns wanting
     song
       lines

Statue Man

Wooden man
yes man
runs down the hill
and back again
black fox leaping at his heels

Yes sir, yes sir
whatever you say
meat and potatoes
daily bread
spectre strokes chill fingers
                      down
                      his
                      spine

Fleeing
through sleeping streets
runs statue man
wind at his back
thin spirit
moves with his black twin
escape meat body
        yes man
                yes

History

My friend, you walk a thin line
invisible to a casual eye
neck muscles rigid cords
teeth clench
toes grip
your way is the knife edge
along an abyss
While blood thunders
his voice insinuates
his-story
revisionism ensnares
feet fumble on
razor-back ridge
no safe ground to either side
your truth
his truth
hiss
story
They say if you fall
your partner at his end of the rope
should fling himself the other way
a just balance
if the rope holds
But your tormentor
would leap your way
Down you would go
lashed together
unstoppable unspeakable
repeating history.

KUMQUAT
Poems

Separate Cages

In my widow's cage alone
in a bed for two
eyes open in the darkness
I picture you.
Perhaps you are awake
Saturday Night Blues
the midnight hour
winding down on your radio
(your pink wife in facial cream
asleep)
thinking of me.
You in your marriage cage
a long and solid one,
Me in my widow's cage
a cold and empty one
joined this night
by the rhythm of the blues.
Our mutual habit of replaying
each nuance
word
unspoken,
to face each morning irritable
in separated houses
bags under our eyes.

Two Rings

Two rings speak your eternal promise
paired side-by-side in your long
march to the ark or the urn,
yoked rings the handcuffs
that keep your hands from mine
I'm sidelined from this trek
ringless.
Ashes in a box
betray my promise
I'm cuffed to a spectre
looking on
you two-step by.
Though your eyes lock mine
our hearts pound in unison
the air is as warm as syrup,
go
to your chosen fate
no word or kiss.
You cannot speak
with this ring in your tongue
I will not speak
betray your promise
as I have been betrayed.

Dreaming in Colour

If I could invite him to my bed
cold as brass
steal from his warm wife
to this solitary
room to tinker with ice
red and yellow paintings
stacked around walls
grey for him.
Half a closet
half a hole
heart a hole
cupped in chilled fingers
cage of my heart.
I dream of colour
where touch is possible
yellow hay in a corner field
grey clouds heavy over a school
red oils under artificial light
motel room in the purple dark.
Heat of drama eyes lock eyes
lips to lips or nape of neck
pump blood to hot tipped
fingers whole heart
confession relief and
joy.
Images and dreams
cannot shatter the glass
holds this hole
nor remove the ring
pierces his tongue.

Red Flowers

His mother
made these sheets
that swaddle our illegitimate passion
a fact we cannot forget
her excessive red flowers of craziness
part to permit a rational seam
then bloom again
unfocused infanticidal profusion
obsession enacted by her son
ensnared in her vines
lips stained red with strawberries
red flowers bursting in his brain
Welcome clear colourless vision
to wash this stain
memoirs written in blood
reclaim the colour red or green or grey
for passion.

Following the Rules

No cheap pine box
this marriage
but doublewide
solid mahogany.
I come to the viewing
silver anniversary open casket
detect your pounding heart
despite your still white form
your eyes speak
you are voiceless.
She moves to you
frilly tick or squid
tentacle arms to hold you.
As other woman
I throw rice.
On the shoulders of your community
you pass on to your fiftieth.
Congratulations.

Kumquat

illicit kumquat
sweet and bitter
so tiny
tempts yet more greedy passion
each nibble a commitment
to another bigger bite
love too exotic
for mundane everyday
hopeless to disguise it as
an orange

Hopeless Hope

Hope lost
hurts less than hopeless hope.
I have dwelled in a house of hope
with you
our craftman's collaboration
of intimating words
your turn my turn your turn mine;
I thought we were negotiating
our future.
I have shrugged off hope
not a house of dreams
just a game of words.
Love or
together or
I'll leave my wife for you
never said.
I turn my back on
the house that never was
alone
bleak plain of pain
see behind in my mind's eye
myself
paused in flight
wild-eyed
one foot inside the hoping heart
but turned to face
that lonely place landscaped
by cold reason.
Frozen
in hopeless hope
unspoken love
as final as death.

Exchange

A bowl
confesses perfection
its round holding
a red rose floating
at the heart
my heart a cooked chicken
in peasants' heavy earthenware
pot of dirt
midnight glazed
no stars twinkle romance
a simple exchange
instead of love
I give you this blue pot
Thank-you
Good-bye

Mixed MESSAGES #3

Troll

Mad troll dances
round lumpish potato
companion wind a wild dervish
to run from this guilt
– pointless
he stays in symbiotic step
big boots dance holes
in my soul
sprouts for stupid eyes
wind insists confusion
No rest.

Boundaries

       thin line
lay me on the line
he laid it on the line
he laid me on the line
boundaries
binder twine
bound in twain
lines crossed
I'm telling lies
       thin lies
binding words spoken
broken on this wheel
circle endless line
endless lies entwine
embrace
brace for the embrace
save face
face life
       thin life
think life
entwined in this embrace
bound to this place
I untie the line
leave a living lie
trace a new line
I define the space
embrace boundaries
work the margins
I draw the line
       firm line

Giving Voice

Today I read Freire
Young son writes
Friend burns poems

      dansn god [dancing god]
      clod god [cloud god]
      "and these three are ghosts"

Action, reflection
I name my world
create myself: writer's work
a being and becoming

      magik god [magic god]
      butifl god [beautiful god]
      goblin guy

She kneels at home hearth
in hot rage
feeds the fire
each flaming poem a suicide
self mutilation, capitulation
words to ash

I will no longer fight
I will fit into a box
I will let oppressors name me
I will burn my generative words

life
lifework consumed
cremated

    war god
    wotr god [water god]
    gost madin [ghost maiden]

Mommy Medusa

Mommy Medusa
tie up that hair.

Strangled snakes don't speak
Limp tongues red hair ribbons.

Fold hands
Cross ankles
Turn eyes inward.

A presentable woman
good Wife.

List of Rules

My theory of dishwashers:
you can always cram in one more
cup fork spatula
but never cover the middle fountain
or do the whole damn load again.
My space-time continuum theory:
it takes zero time to get from point A to B
with a vanload of kids.
I'm habitually late.
Headful of lists:
household chores
yard work, repairs, groceries
schedules for lessons, sports and school
endless urgent lists at work.
I need the rules
to manage the lists
that constitute my life.
(Cruel magazine image:
smiling model in loungewear
cheek to cheek with adoring stud
sipping wine in the sun porch
of her immaculate log home.
She looks well-rested.)
I'm running down my list:
email – check
write report – check
daughter to doctor – check.
I multitask: mark papers in the waiting room
draft report while driving
plan dinner as I scrub the floor.

No spontaneous moments of joy
for this automaton
her middle fountain quenched
doomed to construct lists
and live them out at light speed
without raising her head
sniffing the air
mommy machine
can do it all.

Still Shots

Time tableaux
of still shots
sequence of eternal nows
until this moment
mottled, toothless.

Firm youth taunts
irretrievable, slips
to slippers
blinks
memory's mercurial lens.

Rushing
to here and here
ends at night's window
shade of deadman
reflected in my shape
wide-eyed mirror.

Ripe woman
holds the child, the spectre
interred internal
static pose.

Colour

A traditionalist
in his monochromatic world
follows rules: value study.
Grid transfer replicates
black & white detail
shades of grey, a concession.
Only then, a stingy measure of colour
layered over deadening black
understated sepia mud
his careful copywork.

The impressionist
paints passion
slaps it on, wet & thick.
Some painter, giddy with colour
has taken her tube of cerulean
and, against all reason,
declared the sky blue.
She invests pigment
dares to insist on magenta shadows
pink impasto ticks of light.

Against complements dark
light vibrates.

September Eleventh

stopped in time
today's texture tasteless, touchless
an envelope for waiting
eyes on my electronic feed
historic moment an interstice of nothingness
interminable empty stretch
knowing nothing
nothing
ever to be the same
as yesterday's yolk yellow
safe sane days
not knowing what happens after
the first day of war
or what to do with my hands
the world as we know it
ends

Slipping Inside

Fragments
prismatic image-shifts
your focus flicks to doubles,
uncertain boundaries
(until the uncertainty of everything
itself obsesses)
flustered
fracturing.

And I see from your troubled eyes
that try to hold mine
but turn within,
my voice is barely audible
in your internal din.

Those me-tentacles
stranglehold you,
other recedes;
the effort to disambiguate
shifting doubles – too much.

Slipping out of normalcy
reality redefines
memories, events reconstruct
re-construe. . .
no warrant
no hook to hang one version on.

All this I can see
and you cannot
my voice a lone bean rattling
among ghosts
shifting through your landscape.

I Am Old

A young man
eyes as light and bright as the horizon
California hair
colour of summer straw.

But I am old,
last week's curled meat
chewed-over gristle
stale and grey.

Alpine hemlock
twisted and tired
wind-hobbled, winter-shrunk
gnarled and hard.

Yet my girlish soul starts
as liquid and frisky as spring run-off
bubbles down mountain meadows,
black rock,

to meet his upturned
innocent words.

Broken Dishes

Too frugal to break dishes, secretly
I smile
as my son smashes the last
unbreakably ugly corningware plate
its skim-milk white thin with
seventies orange trim
garbage-canned shards.
No fond memories
of the 40 below Regina Army & Navy
student loan poverty
that contextualized the purchase.
Only the remnants of two
mismatched cheap
stoneware sets missing mostly
bowls
from the saving for a house
hungry single mother
years
to go.
With kids accidentally dropping
dishes, chili, ice cream, cups
I'll soon be down to saucers
irrelevant to kids
too useless even for garage sales
to store forever more on the
ironically safe
unreachable
top shelf.
Cupless, plateless

I'll go buy
whimsical sunflowers on an impressionist's sky
hand-painted four place
setting
for my alone-ly
no kids to break things
empty nest.
Just me, my dishes, and
those damned resilient saucers
shelved
out of sight.

Travelling Forward

small woman in black
leans into a wall of wind
or strains to pull
a stone sledge laden with bones
red rags
mouths whispering ma
ma

or bends low
over a bicycle
ropey arms
neck cords like telephone wires
pedalling against time
tears flatten on temples
stream behind –
concentration potholes
in blacktop thin as eggshells
sudden circles
deep as China
break axles, ankles
up to the armpits
in the honeycombed labyrinth
of a freeze/thaw brain

thin edge Twister game
safety lacks handholds
on a scaffold of forward march
over the bottomless pit
where all the wolves that ever were
swarm through regret's graveyard
moist red lips
tongues raspy with glue

still she toils
unravelling as she goes
a history of blue arteries, red veins
bind the little bird
stone sledge
too heavy for hollow bones
dry straws sent tumbling
in the morning breath
of tomorrow's unknown
bedfellows

POINTS
North

Written-Upon Woman

I am the written-upon woman
it started with hands
milk
bread
phone the dentist
white hands flutter
in front.
I walk
in weed-edged streets
behind strip malls,
warehouses
where the poor of North America
watch big TVs
in stucco bungalows
drinking Lucky
smoking Luckies.
Torn plastic flaps,
invites flies
crooked against dirt-speckled pane
sun, white heat.
Highway trucks,
one and another, roar
these hands flutter
leaves on a breeze
stir diesel fumes and dust.
Written-on wrists
existentialism
surgery
on the temples
language

look up Wittgenstein.
On the inner thighs
crude cartoons.
The hands, blue ballpoint veins
claw hot air.
Game-shows clamour
write their babble.
Burrs in my bobby socks
milkweed gone to seed
I can't whiteout plastic curtains
rethink stucco
banish trucks.
I am the written-upon woman
lucky.

Valley Of My Childhood

Coming south from the Yukon border
1000 miles of dust and potholes
windshield greasy with bugs,
I emerge from the bush at Kitwanga
to the valley of my childhood,
not civilization after all –
more of the same.
Ragged edges.
Maidens,
skin green as poplar bark
reach out with trembling wrists.
Knee-deep
weeds run up the ditch
claw crumbles of blacktop.
Fireweed, paintbrush, sweet clover, yarrow
in painterly clumps.
Shadowed
devil's club and skunk cabbage
soak roots in acid soil,
harbour mosquitoes.
With a stranger's eyes I see
this secondary highway
tar-patched by men in pavement trucks
losing against the bush.
Ephemeral,
my home.
Pop machines and parking lots
a temporary dream.
River, rocks, trees, and weeds
resist,

persist.
When I am 90
babbling northern valley memories
in my city care-home bed,
roads will have returned to bush
tall trees will shake their silver crowns
white towers mounting a blue sky
bright river
running down a trackless valley.
Memory an old woman's tale
disconfirmed.

December 25

huckleberry smudge of dying sun
salmon iced peaks
I at riparian boundary
winter creek
black waters
deep bowl
rimmed by mountains
twilight of the festival of light

Sculpture

Black fingers fracture light
crooked elbows, many limbs
bunched bundles of twigs outstretch
frame a sculpture of cloud mass, light panes.
Living scaffold
sky structure
shapes our vision –
puffballs on prongs
angled portals of watery light.
Below, toes reach into loam
wrap around boulders
nematode roots
suck liquid up to thin bright air
where leaf cutouts clatter and pose
shiny side up.
Enfolded in scabbed skin
deep in the woody flesh
life's movement,
bittersweet nourishment
slow as the breath
of soil, water, light, air.
Also moving upwards
an undulation of caterpillars
scorned by birds
who dip and soar
in negative space
behind a wooden tangle
of sky windows.

Left Behind

Last day in October
already November trees
steadfast charcoal tracery
against thin yellow light
panorama of upswept cloud
that surprising fragile blue of northern skies.

In her milltown, further north
Kathie teaches
blocking until dismissal, thoughts
of daughter's schedule, dog to vet
incomplete thesis waiting
– bread baking, reading, writing, crafts,
crackling log in woodstove –
nostalgias firmly pressed down.

Lynda drives across Vancouver
stop and start city traffic
on her cell phone handling office crises,
daycare, physio, dinner, tickets
no time to raise her eyes
where gulls wheel and call
above freighters in the blue ocean,
white puffball clouds
scud toward mountains.

Sarah on the Island
home sick this day
pantyhose abandoned
plans gluten-free meals

waits for teenagers
to get off the phone
– the log cabin in Salmon Valley
rented to strangers
kayaks still in storage
plants left behind are withering.

Ana, on her apartment balcony
in New Orleans, lush and green
sips scotch, watches with her cats
Canadian birds
that northern bush, her lakeside home
lost.

Diane, on the east coast
dutiful daughter heeds the call
family health emergency
from tropical exile to a purgatory
of nuances, unfinished stories
footloose, cut free
wooden home in a pine forest sold
homeless,
rudderless.

I'm still here
shifting spirits picture my landscape
encapsulated, embittered, excommunicated
I see them sideways
imagination's window
so close
so distant through wavering glass.

Bees Among the Canes

Fat orange bee
works the raspberry blooms
with her smaller sisters.
My grandmother's canes
from her pioneer farm
to the Main Street house
in the railway town
where she died;
to my father's plot
to me, now sadly overgrown.
The cat comes yawning and smiling
from long grass under the apple tree.
A lacework of tiny flies
decorates the dapple of ankle-deep
lawn, mower a greasy heap
of broken parts.
Gulps of wind lightly lift
leaves of poplar, pulsing, shushing
bees among the swaying canes
and I suddenly know
we'll make it.

Stolen Moment

A moment as polished, round, and blue
as the cobalt lake below
amoeba arms enfold wheat yellow grass
red willow, ragweed
the rhythm of aspen and hills
October's cadmium colours
a circular silence opens.

Above on the rocky overlook
field-trip preteens in motion
restless as a hilltop breeze
surge to the edge
behind grey stump and tree
eating, talking, leaping, talking
an energy of social couplings
physical flow over and through
the landscape, imperceptive
like the adults apart, converse.

This day a comma
in the black and white checklist
everyday's relentless time clock.

Haiku for October

iridescent beads
polished autumn days distilled
precious finite count

Restless Feet

Always these restless northern feet
running a bush path
toes seek its turns
muddy soft spots, roots
wet willow, white fireweed, nettle
mottled autumn cranberry
their acrid crimson odor.

And why do I have this restless mind
unpicking, resticking?
Grip slippery words
inflated, related
twist wordy slips
wrest theirs and mine.
Mis
re:
present
ation, oration, relation.
Think!

And these greedy eyes
cerulean swatch
lemon long late rays
umber slash of bark
lavender tips.

A beauty of movement
too intense
to rest
lest death impress.

November Grey and Black

November grey and black
subtle pearly patches
horizon's pale peach slip
underpaints black bristle
up-pointing
leafless, loveless trees
still as crystal
cold as forever.

Minimalist landscape
a celebration of tenacity
that even in this silence of muted greys
black etchings
memory as thin as dissipated smoke
are bones of trees
a temple of branches housing a flock
yellow and black
rosy throat birds.

Three brown leaves
beating like hearts
their tiny fluttering wish to fly
fills this moment,
summer's colourful hot rushing
as blurry old as black & white
frames crackled, speechless
in this still reality
November's chill endpoint.

In a Swamp

Jayne spent Christmas in a swamp.
      Until I was five,
      King Street ended at Blackmores' house
      forbidden swamp beyond
      downtown on the other side.
      Barefoot, I ran down the hill
      road sticky with summer tar
      to keep down the dust
      picking sewer flowers from the ditch –
      now I call them chamomile.
They built a road through that swamp
so I could walk through
to grade one.
Straight down the middle
run, Dick, run
"If I ever catch you playing in that swamp,
you'll get the belt when you get home."
      When I was seven
      mean Rich-Jean
      showed off sliding on thin ice
      in new Christmas boots
      fell through, up to her neck.
      We pulled her out
      she cried all the way home to the top of the hill
      trailing black water and mud.
Summers, we caught pollywogs
took them home to turn into frogs
in a washtub under the willow tree.
Moss on fallen logs was four inches thick
a creampuff mattress for viewing clouds.

      Age eleven
      five stitches in my foot
      and a rusty can tetanus shot
      from barefoot tag in a meadow
      under long sun
      when the muck dried up.
The summer I was twelve
they drained the swamp, built the mall town-side
(where I was to have my first job
ringing in canned peas, tripe).
We built a trail through the now-accessible bush
to the high school
much quicker than going around by the road.
      In adulthood
      King Street has been demoted to Prince Street
      there are no more tadpoles.
      I have learned
      the middle letter of the alphabet
      is not all-the-men-go-pee,
      Rich-Jean was named Regine
      and mom stood at the end of our driveway
      up the hill
      shading her eyes with her hand
      to see me through the swamp un-drowned.
Now forty-five, visiting
same house, same town, same used-to-be-swamp
Blackmores' house still there, still brown.
My friend Jayne from Ontario
coincidently visiting too
notices there is no Toronto Dominion Bank
a guest in the new apartment building
built behind the mall twenty years ago
she writes poems
in my remembered swamp.

Erasures

A tree blazed forty years ago
I return by tangled trails:

Brown-eyed woman in a brown housedress
deep in the velvet armchair
knits red ski socks; offers cookies and pies
so happy to see the clever children
of her Jimmy.

No memory of her voice
my child's mind
heard no accent
never learned the mother tongue.

After the funeral
the house on Main Street
crowded with southern aunts
my eyes on Grandma's empty chair
while the shy cat, Tiny,
afraid of children,
slunk behind the woodstove.

Forty years I hear stories.
She lived in a tent
first winter at forty below
raised seven kids in rubber boots
ran three farms
boarded the teacher
cooked for the hotel
buried babies in the Old Country.

It is only in the last twenty
her son
admits his name is not French
respells it without yelling
permits a wooden nameplate
on his door.

Bush trails now are highways
three farms sold
her house torn down
for a Mr. Mikes.

Wearing city shoes
speaking big city words
I return to what I know:
Woman in a brown dress.